This notebook belongs to:

____

Made in the USA
Monee, IL
13 January 2023

25248505R00069